SOUTH WEST
TO THE SEA

ON

Crowns Mine, Botallack

On this wild headland miners once descended to a workplace 1,000 metres beneath the raging waves. Eleven engines were working here in 1865, and men worked in eight-hour shifts, crawling on all fours.

The Tamar Bridges, Saltash

Until Brunel, Cornwall was virtually an island, cut off by the River Tamar. Today, a modern road bridge stands beside his triumph of Victorian engineering.

Harvest from the sea

For centuries the pilchard was the mainstay of the south-west's fishing fleets. Today crab, lobster and crayfish are the main catch of the smaller ports.

$\mathcal{A}$ LAND STEEPED IN HISTORY

Signs of the first footfall date from around 3000 BC. Flint spears and bone artefacts are all that remain of the early Stone Age population, who cleared the wildwood and built their mysterious henge monuments. The Celts dominated the region from the seventh century BC, trading tin with the Phoenicians in exchange for oil and wine, and even when the Romans arrived in the first century AD, they made little impression beyond the Tamar. Celtic rule lasted until the eighth century AD, when the Anglo-Saxons overran the land, but some Celtic institutions still managed to survive in the remoter parts of Cornwall.

After the Norman Conquest, society and culture changed drastically, with the building of castles and churches. In 1337 Edward III created the Duchy of Cornwall as an estate for his eldest son, Edward the Black Prince. The region prospered in the fifteenth century thanks to tin mining and the wool trade, and the establishment of the naval dockyard in Plymouth in the late seventeenth century gave the region national prominence. With the later improvement in roads and railways came the area's most important and lasting source of revenue today – the tourist.

St Senera

The twelfth-century church at Zennor is built on the site of another church founded by a Celtic saint. According to legend, St Senera was the beautiful Princess Asenora, who was accused of infidelity and cast into the sea in a barrel. She arrived in Ireland, and founded the parish of Zennor on her journey home to Brittany, *c*. AD 600.

Methodism amongst the miners

The mining community was deeply religious. This natural hollow in Gwennap was converted to an amphitheatre by miners who flocked to hear John Wesley preach. Methodists from around the world attend the Whit Monday service each year.

Norman relic

The parish churches of the south-west have a fine ecclesiastical legacy. This Norman girdle font (one of twelve in Devon) can be found in St Andrew's, Harberton.

Prehistoric tombs

Lanyon Quoit in the parish of Madron, Cornwall, dates from 2500 BC. An exposed, Neolithic chambered tomb, originally covered by an earth mound, it consists of a massive capstone and three uprights.

Okehampton Castle

This eleventh-century fortification was built by the Normans to guard the road from Cornwall to the east when they created the market town of Okehampton on the northern edge of Dartmoor.

Celtic staging posts

Small Celtic crosses were used to mark resting places on the path of a funeral procession and can be found all over Cornwall.

Clapper bridge, Dartmoor

Constructed from huge slabs of granite, clapper bridges date from the thirteenth century. They allowed heavily laden pack horses to cross swollen rivers in winter.

Relic from the Iron Age

The ruins of eight cottages are all that remain of the ancient village of Chysauster, north-east of Penzance. It was finally abandoned in the third century AD.

Craft of the potter

Tourism is now the chief industry of the south-west, but many of the old crafts continue. Devon and Cornwall are rich in supplies of natural clay and the earliest examples of south-west pottery date from the Bronze Age. Today it thrives as a cottage industry throughout both counties, ranging from everyday objects such as Lamorna Cove tableware to connoisseur pieces such as this unusual clock made by Hemyock potter, Ross Emerson.

Grand Western Canal

The Burlescombe to Tiverton branch opened in 1814 and in 1838 a narrower channel was cut through to Taunton. The aim, to carry goods traffic between south Devon and Bristol, was never realised. It is now a quiet backwater plied by horse-drawn passenger bus.

MEMORIALS TO COURAGE

As long ago as 1800 BC people had learned to blend ore washed down from the south-west's granite heights with Irish copper ore to make bronze. The practice continued to flourish until the Charter of Stannaries, as the tin industry was known, was drawn up in the twelfth century. Alone of the labouring classes the tinner became a free artisan, able to search for tin on any waste land, paying only a toll to the lord of the manor. Stannary towns were set up at Liskeard, Lostwithiel, Truro and Helston in Cornwall, and at Chagford, Lydford, Ashburton, Plympton and Tavistock in Devon. Here, after smelting, the tin was weighed, taxed, stamped with the Duchy arms and sold on to traders from all over Europe. Surface mining continued until the mid-fifteenth century, by which time surface tin was all but exhausted. Over the next 500 years tinners had to dig deeper and deeper to find the ore. With the coming of the Industrial Revolution the south-west's rich deposits of tin, copper, coal and iron brought increased prosperity, and remnants of nineteenth-century industrial activity can be found all over the south-west. South of St Ives is a landscape to rival the drama of Tintagel: a moorland wilderness pitted with the gaunt ruins of what was once the proud Cornish tin mining industry.

Wheal Coates engine house, near St Agnes Head

Coleridge of Ottery St Mary

Son of the local vicar, the English poet Samuel Taylor Coleridge was born in 1772 and baptised in the parish church of Ottery St Mary. A plaque to his memory shows the albatross from his most famous poem, *The Ancient Mariner*.

Frenchman's Creek

Of all twentieth-century writers, no one evokes the spirit of Cornwall better than Daphne du Maurier. She spent most of her life in Cornwall and immortalised the landscape in such novels as *Frenchman's Creek*, set around the Helford Passage.

*T*ELLERS OF TALES

Who better to tell the story than the storytellers? Generations of England's best-loved writers have fallen under the spell of the south-west. Charles Kingsley was the first, with his thrilling adventure story, *Westward Ho!*, in which he describes the treacherous Shutter Rock on the Atlantic coast as 'a huge black fang, waiting for its prey'. In 1848 Lord Alfred Tennyson was inspired to write his Arthurian cycle after visiting Tintagel, while Sir Arthur Conan Doyle based *The Hound of the Baskervilles* (1902) around the legend of the fire-breathing dogs of Dartmoor. Virginia Woolf drew on childhood memories of holidays in St Ives for one of her best novels, *To the Lighthouse* (1927). Today the tradition continues with Mary Wesley, who has set five of her nine best-selling novels in the south-west.

Henry Williamson's otter

For many decades pollution has threatened the environment of this beautiful, rare creature, known to thousands through Henry Williamson's *Tarka the Otter*. The author based the story on his knowledge of north Devon streams.

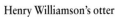

Honeymoon haven

In the beautiful fishing village of Lynmouth in north Devon, today's visitors can rent the cottage where Shelley spent his honeymoon with sixteen-year-old Harriet Westbrook in 1812.

Watersmeet, Exmoor

Exmoor will forever be associated with RD Blackmore's romantic novel, *Lorna Doone*. What better place for a lovers' tryst than the deep, wooded gorge pictured here where Hoar Oak Water runs into the East Lyn River?

Charles Dickens's Clovelly

Famous for its steep, pedestrian street, Clovelly has changed little since Charles Dickens visited it in 1860. It appeared as 'Steepways' in his Christmas story of that year, co-written with his travelling companion Wilkie Collins. In the nineteenth century popular writers such as Dickens, Collins, Wordsworth and Coleridge were instrumental in introducing their readers to the more inaccessible parts of the south-west, such as Clovelly, Lynmouth and Penzance.

Queen of mystery

Born in Torquay, Dame Agatha Christie wrote over seventy classic detective novels. In Torre Abbey, Torquay, used as Torbay Council's Fine Art Gallery and Museum, a room furnished with her possessions has been set up as a memorial.

Looking south towards Brendon Common, Exmoor

Watersmeet, Exmoor

NORTH DEVON
RUGGED COAST AND MOORLAND

In the east, Exmoor advances majestically to the sea; lacking either bogs or mires, this is a friendly wilderness, mile upon mile of fertile pasture melting into moor. Heather-covered heights, deep ravines and tumbling waterfalls characterise this most romantic of landscapes. Blackmore based his classic novel *Lorna Doone* on a real-life family of bandits who terrorised the district in the seventeenth century. Today, pony trekkers explore Exmoor's delights on ancient bridle paths, undisturbed except for the call of the pied flycatcher, the stonechat and the wagtail. To the west, north Devon's pride is miles of glorious golden beaches where the resorts of Ilfracombe, Westward Ho! and Woolacombe have played host to generations of holidaymakers.

Barnstaple – a country town . . .

The bustling market town of Barnstaple began life as a Saxon village. Given its charter in AD 930, it is one of England's oldest burghs. Six centuries separate the graceful arches of its medieval Long Bridge from those of the early Victorian Pannier Market, still in use today.

Route to the top

Sir George Newnes built this funicular railway which climbs the vertical cliff-face to join Lynton above with its sister village Lynmouth, 150 metres below.

. . . and a town of strong naval traditions

A statue of Queen Anne stands atop the colonnade of Queen Anne's walk, the elegant eighteenth-century trading exchange that once faced the busy quay. Deals used to be settled across the Tome Stone in the presence of a witness, without signing contracts. Built at the lowest point where it is possible to bridge the River Taw, Barnstaple was a thriving port until the river silted up. In 1588, five ships, the *Dudley*, the *Tiger*, the *John of Barnstaple*, the *Unicorn* and the *God Save Her*, sailed from Barnstaple to join Sir Francis Drake's fleet against the Spanish Armada.

A ride back in time

Built in 1820, Arlington Court was the home of the Chichester family until the death of Miss Rosemary Chichester in 1949. An ardent collector, Miss Chichester acquired many small objets d'art, but her overriding passion was for wildlife. In the grounds she created a nature reserve where Jacob sheep and Shetland ponies still roam. Arlington Court also has a fine collection of horse-drawn vehicles; the carriage shown here is drawn by Hercules and Mr Cobbler.

Timekeeper

This fine example of a rare tavern clock is a relic from the days of clock tax, when customers paid a levy on their ale towards the tax. The painting on the face is a faithful rendition of the view across Lynmouth bay.

Picturesque Clovelly

One of Devon's most popular villages, Clovelly is famous for its single cobbled street, 'Up-a-long Down-a-long', that plummets to the sea. Donkeys no longer bear the brunt of hauling goods, but Clovelly is strictly pedestrians only, thanks to landowner Christine Hamlyn, who vowed to keep the village unspoiled. For the weak of limb, the estate landrover transports passengers on a back road between the visitors' centre at the top and the harbour at the bottom.

Travellers' rest

The archetypal Devon hostelry catches the early rays of sunrise on a summer morning. The Rising Sun overlooks the harbour of the small fishing village of Lynmouth on the edge of Exmoor. For 500 years travellers have slept snug beneath its thatch, waking to the view of boats bobbing in the harbour and the Rhenish Tower, a folly built upon the pier. It is said that RD Blackmore lodged here while he wrote *Lorna Doone*; the inn is a mere six miles across Exmoor from the ill-fated Doone Valley of his novel.

LUNDY – PUFFIN ISLAND

The name of this tiny granite island, twelve miles off the north Devon coast across Bideford Bay, is Norse for 'Island of Puffins'. Sadly, the puffin population has dwindled to twenty pairs, in part due to the predatory activities of the rare British mammal, the black rat. At night, puffins roost at sea, leaving their eggs and young unprotected in their burrows. *Rattus rattus* arrived on these shores around the fourth century and can now only be found in four British locations: Dundee, the Western Isles, Alderney and Lundy. Due to its rarity, and its extreme shyness, the black rat population has been left undisturbed. Despite Lundy's size, no more than half a mile by three miles, the island has a colourful past: in its time, it has provided refuge for all manner of villains, from pirates to smugglers. Now owned by the National Trust, it is administered by the Landmark Trust, and is a haven for nature lovers and bird watchers instead.

Dartmoor
THE LAST GREAT ENGLISH WILDERNESS

Five granite masses form the backbone of the south-west. At the heart of Devon, Dartmoor is the highest and the largest, stretching for 330 square miles. It has an astonishing legacy of prehistoric monuments, standing stones, burial tombs and over 1,500 granite hut circles, which were once the homes of Dartmoor's Bronze Age inhabitants. Then it was much warmer, and the whole area was more conducive to settlement, with an abundance of building stones and supply of fresh water. Since the first millennium BC, however, climatic change and soil exhaustion have given rise to the desolate, peat-covered wilderness we see today.

The first mention of Dartmoor was in 1181 when it was called Dertemora. Tin mining took hold during the twelfth century, when it became the prime source of tin in Europe. In 1337, Edward III granted it to the Black Prince, the first Duke of Cornwall, and it has been part of the Duchy of Cornwall ever since. Made a national park in 1951, the moor is popular with walkers and pony trekkers who follow the paths made by medieval pack horses.

Castle Drogo

A summer display in the grounds of Sir Edwin Lutyens's granite masterpiece, which overlooks the Teign gorge in north-east Dartmoor. The castle took twenty years to complete (between 1910 and 1930) and was the last of its kind to be built in England. The name comes from the lord of the manor in the days of Richard I.

Bronze Age monument

In prehistoric times, burial grounds were places of superstition and fear. A stone circle often enclosed the place of burial. There are twelve circles on Dartmoor. On the northern moor, the stone circle at Scorhill, near Gidleigh, with twenty-three upright stones, is one of the most atmospheric.

Dartmoor ponies

The pure-bred Dartmoor pony is descended from stock brought to England by the Iron Age Celts. The 2,500 ponies that wander the moor today are cross-breeds; delightful to look at, they can be skittish and should be treated with caution.

Vixen Tor

Old English for 'heap', a tor is a high, rocky outcrop, found all over the moors of the south-west. Every year thousands of youngsters come from all over the country to take part in the Ten Tors Walk, organised by the Army. Standing thirty metres high from the ground, Vixen, often called the Sphinx, is the tallest.

Buckland-in-the-Moor

An enchanting hamlet at the heart of the moor where Ruddycleave Water plunges 120 metres to the River Dart.

Life force of the moor

The River Dart is one of the fourteen rivers that became crucial to the economy of the moor. In the late fifteenth century, this river was used to revolutionise the production of wool: specially designed mills built near fast-flowing rivers speeded up the process of 'fulling' (cleaning and thickening) the wool. Wealthy clothiers financed the entire enterprise from growing the wool on the sheep's back to the production of the finished cloth, which was then exported abroad.

Widecombe-in-the-Moor

Immortalised in the folk song *Widecombe Fair*, when 'Uncle Tom Cobbleigh and all' borrowed Tom Pearce's grey mare to ride to Widecombe Fair from Sticklepath, the village of Widecombe is set in the heart of Dartmoor. From the thirteenth century every track from the south and east led to Widecombe Church, known as 'the cathedral of the moor' because of its unusually high spire.

A view of the churchyard, Buckland-in-the- Moor

The clock at St Peter's, Buckland-in-the-Moor

The letters on the clock face, starting from nine o'clock, read 'My Dear Mother', a tribute from Mr Whitley, a former lord of the manor.

Haytor Rock

One of the most frequented destinations on the moor, Haytor Rock stands at 457 metres above sea level. Its accessibility, being close to the road, and the fact that it is an easy climb, have made it popular with generations of climbers.

Writers' retreat

Built around an octagonal, turreted market house, Chagford is one of Devon's stannary towns, set up in the twelfth century to administer the tin mining industry. In 1945, following Cyril Connelly's advice, that the writer's 'rightful place of composition is the small, single unluxurious retreat of the twentieth century, the hotel bedroom', Evelyn Waugh moved into Easton Court, a Chagford hotel whose PEN Club advertisement described it as 'understanding writers' needs' and whose telegraphic address was 'nanny'. Evelyn Waugh's resulting book was *Brideshead Revisited*.

Bowerman's Nose

This natural rock formation, at seven metres tall, is said to be a local man turned to stone for the sin of hunting on the Sabbath.

Dartmoor sheep

Sheep have always been the most numerous livestock on Dartmoor. In the early nineteenth century there were 14,000 in the parish of Widecombe alone. The Dartmoor sheep is one of the few breeds able to survive Dartmoor's harsh winters. It is placid by nature – it is said that when faced with an obstacle, it will simply sit down and wait for it to go away.

Domesday village

An ancient, steep, winding track leads down from the suburbs of Torquay to Cockington. With their steeply pitched, thatched roofs and pastel-pink walls, the cottages of this delightful hamlet provide a story-book setting. The Domesday Book of 1086 describes the site as 'land for 13 ploughs ... with 15 acres of meadow, 50 acres of pasture and 50 acres of woods.' By the 1659 survey, Cockington had grown somewhat, housing 200 people (mostly farm workers) in thirty-seven cottages. When designing the Drum Inn in 1920, Sir Edwin Lutyens took care to blend it in with the village vernacular. Today Cockington Valley is owned by Torbay Borough Council, who manage it as a country park.

A pastoral scene - somewhere between Dartmouth and Totnes.

SOUTH DEVON
GREEN VALES WITH A STRONG MARITIME TRADITION

Imagine a rolling patchwork of hills and deep wooded valleys, punctuated with hamlets and historic market towns. Colour it green, for here the vegetation is lush and almost sub-tropical. On a winding lane a flock of Devon long-hairs may slow the motorist to a crawl as they gambol along, sun-speckled fleece and tails abobbing.

Along the coast of south Devon are places that have become synonymous with summer holidays: the Regency resorts of Sidmouth, Exmouth and Budleigh Salterton; Torquay and Paignton, grand dames of the English Riviera; bustling Brixham and Salcombe, the yachting haven; and Bigbury-on-Sea with nearby Burgh Island whose hotel was once a favourite with the *haute monde* of the 1920s. Finally, the coast curves round to the historic site that has been the starting point of so many English naval triumphs, Plymouth Sound.

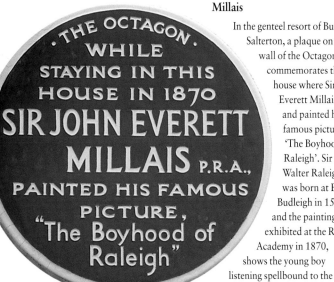

Regency splendour

The elegance of Sidmouth's Regency esplanade ends abruptly in towering cliffs of sandstone. As a baby, Queen Victoria was taken for her morning constitutional along the sea front by her impoverished father, the Duke of Kent.

Totnes - a crooked town?

The High Street in Totnes is a visual feast of historic buildings, from the charming mock Gothic confection, glimpsed down Bank Lane, to the carved wooden gargoyles (*pictured right*) on the Elizabethan Town House Museum. At the restoration ceremony of the East Gate, which was destroyed by fire in 1990, the crooked setting of the new clock was brought to the attention of the Mayor, who wryly replied, 'No sir, the clock is straight. It is Totnes that's crooked.'

Princess Gardens, Torquay

In the early nineteenth century the Napoleonic Wars curtailed travel to the continent and the first trickle of visitors began to arrive in Devon. Genteel excursionists with easels and water colours were joined by naval families wishing to be near the fleet in Torquay. Today, Torquay's mild temperatures and long hours of sunshine ensure its reputation as the Queen of the English Riviera.

Millais

In the genteel resort of Budleigh Salterton, a plaque on the wall of the Octagon commemorates the house where Sir John Everett Millais lived and painted his famous picture, 'The Boyhood of Raleigh'. Sir Walter Raleigh was born at East Budleigh in 1552 and the painting, exhibited at the Royal Academy in 1870, shows the young boy listening spellbound to the yarns of a fisherman.

Oldway Mansion, Paignton

Versailles was the inspiration for this late nineteenth-century pile. Built as a pleasure retreat for the sewing machine magnate, Isaac Merritt Singer, it is now Paignton's municipal offices.

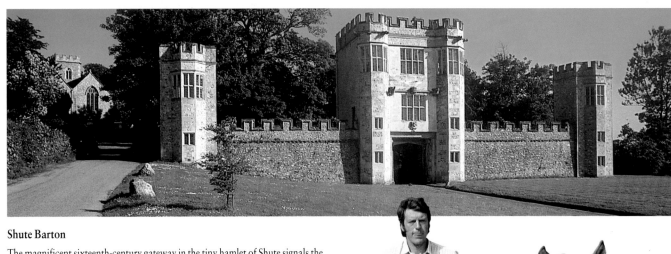

Shute Barton

The magnificent sixteenth-century gateway in the tiny hamlet of Shute signals the grandeur of Shute Barton beyond, one of the best examples of a fortified manor house in Britain, built by Sir William Bonville in 1380.

Four maidens

Detail from a memorial sculpture in St Mary's Church, Totnes.

Return to an old tradition

After almost half a century, once again the ring of horses' hooves is a familiar sound in Devon lanes as farmers, concerned with the effect of modern methods on the environment, forsake them for the trusty cart horse.

A La Ronde, Exmouth

Set on a hillside with magnificent views, A La Ronde is a delightful fantasy: a sixteen-sided, limestone house, created in 1798 by the cousins Jane and Mary Parminter after their visit to San Vitale in Ravenna. Visitors may walk round the inner octagon through a succession of eccentric rooms crammed with curiosities made from shells and feathers, glass and lichen. The Parminters intended that the house should only be inhabited by female descendants, but this plan was thwarted in 1883 when Oswald Reichel inherited the property. It has belonged to the National Trust since 1991.

Dartmouth: ancient port

The Second and Third Crusades sailed from Dartmouth as did the men headed for the beaches of Normandy, 800 years later. Its fifteenth-century castle, pictured here, was the first to be built with proper gun ports, although these have never been put to the test in war. This explains the castle's excellent state of preservation. The actual town of Dartmouth is dominated by the Britannia Royal Naval College, high on a hill.

Surfers' paradise
Wind-surfing at Salcombe – a popular leisure pursuit.

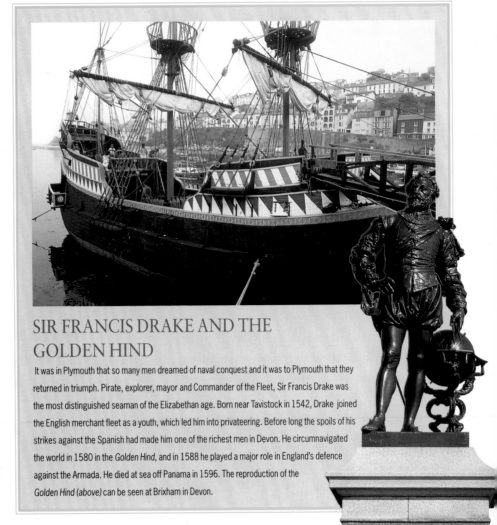

SIR FRANCIS DRAKE AND THE GOLDEN HIND

It was in Plymouth that so many men dreamed of naval conquest and it was to Plymouth that they returned in triumph. Pirate, explorer, mayor and Commander of the Fleet, Sir Francis Drake was the most distinguished seaman of the Elizabethan age. Born near Tavistock in 1542, Drake joined the English merchant fleet as a youth, which led him into privateering. Before long the spoils of his strikes against the Spanish had made him one of the richest men in Devon. He circumnavigated the world in 1580 in the *Golden Hind*, and in 1588 he played a major role in England's defence against the Armada. He died at sea off Panama in 1596. The reproduction of the *Golden Hind* (above) can be seen at Brixham in Devon.

Maritime museum in a Victorian warehouse

The museum's outstanding collection of ships ranges from a Welsh coracle to the state barge used in the film, *A Man for all Seasons*.

The house that moved

In 1961 this delightful house, once the home of a Tudor merchant, found itself in the path of the Exeter ring road. Modern technology allowed it to be moved to its present site opposite Stepcote Hill.

Exeter
THE HUB OF DEVON

The earliest part of Exeter's town wall dates from when the Romans established their frontier town to rule the land they called Dumnonii – Devon and Cornwall. The earliest buildings were of wood, but before the end of the first century AD the first public stone buildings had been constructed. Exeter was heavily bombed in 1942 but miraculously the cathedral escaped and, although a modern city has been built up around it, there are still many features to remind us of Exeter's past. Fore Street, for example, a continuation of the High Street, was once an Iron Age track to the River Exe, while just off this street there is a series of underground aqueducts constructed during the thirteenth century, designed to carry fresh water to the city.

The Georgians were the first to build outside the Roman walls and there are still some elegant Regency and early Victorian houses to be seen, such as the St Olaves Hotel in Mary Arches Street. This was built for James Galsworthy in 1837, after he had saved the townspeople during a typhoid epidemic by allowing them access to the only clean water available, that of the Roman well in his forecourt.

Haunt of Elizabethan sea captains

Looking over the cathedral precinct, the sixteenth-century Ship Inn was popular with Sir Walter Raleigh.

Ship Inn

Mother church of the south-west

Founded by the Normans in 1050, the major part of Exeter Cathedral was completed by 1250. Its Norman towers still dominate the skyline. They are surpassed only by the magnificent west front and the interior main vault. This ninety-metre avenue of Gothic vaulting is the longest in the world.

Theologian

In Cathedral Close, a statue of Richard Hooker, an Exeter-born man and a prominent Elizabethan scholar and theologian, surveys the scene.

Elizabethan favourite

Sir Francis Drake was a regular customer in Mols Coffee house, a finely timbered and gabled building, situated in the Cathedral Close.

Heroes' gallery

The west front of the cathedral was originally conceived as a screen to display some 340 sculpted figures. These ranged from biblical figures to monarchs and saints.

Spanish aspirations

With splendid views across Plymouth Sound, Mount Edgcumbe's Grade I historic garden is the earliest landscaped park in Cornwall. In 1588 it was coveted by no less a personage than Medina Sidonia, commander of the Spanish Armada, who swore it would be his home should he defeat the English. The garden shown here is the immaculately laid out French Garden.

Land of giants

Visitors to Newquay's attraction 'Tunnels Through Time' meet the characters of myth and legend, such as Bolster, the giant with the six-mile stride, who fell in love with the virtuous St Agnes. She cunningly demanded that he fill a great hole in the cliff with his blood and the foolish giant, unaware that the hole was bottomless, bled to death.

CORNISH MOORS AND MYTHS

The north Cornwall coast takes its character from the wild Atlantic. Most travellers approach it from across Bodmin Moor on a route that climbs high above the treacherous bogs, the same route trodden by pack horses for centuries past. Here is a savage beauty, one that should be given the respect it deserves. Cornwall is rich in tales of unwitting travellers, who set out across Bodmin Moor, never to be seen again. Anyone who doubts the perils of the moor should read Daphne du Maurier's terrifying account of becoming lost while riding across Bodmin Moor from Jamaica Inn to North Hill. Her experience that night was to be the inspiration for her famous tale of villainy on Bodmin Moor, *Jamaica Inn*.

Ponies grazing on Bodmin Moor

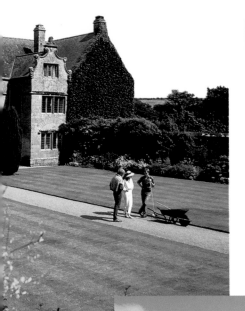

Trerice: Royalist stronghold

This gabled Elizabethan manor house near Newquay, containing original fireplaces and ornate plaster ceilings, was built in 1571. The home of the Arundell family, it is considered to be one of the finest small country houses in Cornwall. In 1646, its owner, Sir John Arundell, defended Pendennis Castle, the last Royalist stronghold to fall, during a five-month siege.

Giant's footsteps

The Bedruthan Steps are said to be the steps of a mighty giant; tales of giants abound in Cornish folklore and may have their origin in the coming of the Celts, who were taller than the native population.

Rough Tor

At 400 metres, this peak is the second highest on Bodmin Moor.

Towan Beach, Newquay

The name Newquay comes from the building of its pier in the fifteenth century. Once a fishing village, Newquay is now Cornwall's premier resort, famous for its golden beaches and dramatic cliff-top scenery. Championship surfing contests are staged here annually.

THE CORNISH COASTAL PATH

The Cornish coastal path runs for 268 miles, making it one of the longest continuous footpaths in England. It begins at Marsland in the north where huge Atlantic breakers crash against the cliffs. Every twist and turn brings new delights: towering headlands, miles of unspoiled beaches and, nestling in tiny creeks and coves, the fishing hamlets with their quaint cottages and inns – Boscastle, Port Isaac and Port Gaverne. At Land's End the path leaves the Atlantic and turns along granite cliffs towards Mousehole, razed by Spanish privateers in 1595. It dips and turns past Penzance to Mount's Bay where, legend has it, a giant created St Michael's Mount. And then the landscape changes; barren cliffs give way to the lush vegetation of the Lizard Peninsula with its gentle network of hidden creeks and wooded river banks – Kynance, Cadgwith and Coverack. Through spring and summer nature shows the way with an unrivalled display of wild flowers: cliff-tops smothered in sea campion, hillsides glowing gold with gorse, and woodland glades carpeted in wild garlic and wood sorrel.

The quintessential fishing village

Port Isaac consists of a cluster of cottages grouped around a tiny harbour where crab and lobster are still landed daily. The tiers of cottages rise higgledy-piggledy up the cliff-face, linked by a series of gravity-defying alleys known as 'drangs' including the famous 'Squeezybelly Alley'. At the height of eighteenth-century smuggling, a complicated series of lantern signals was published here, for distribution to the masters of smuggling vessels. At low tide the harbour doubles as a car park. Absent-minded visitors may return to find their cars have gone out with the tide!

Gateway to Cornwall

Close to the Devon border, the hilltop town of Launceston remained the administrative centre of Cornwall until 1838. Robert of Mortain, the first Earl of Cornwall, ruled from this early motte and bailey, now a public park. Public executions took place here until 1821.

Jamaica Inn

This sign hangs above the portal of the inn at Bolventor where Daphne du Maurier stayed in 1930.

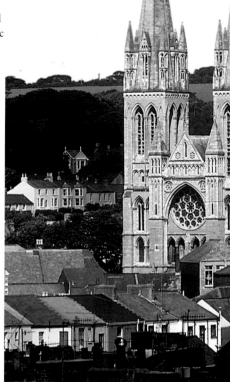

London of the West

Despite being ten miles from the sea, Truro, Cornwall's present administrative centre, was once a thriving medieval port. Its fortunes declined in the seventeenth century, partly due to Charles II's displeasure – the town had given his father scant support during the Civil War. Its heyday came in the nineteenth century when its elegant Georgian architecture earned it the nickname 'London of the West'. Lemon Street is still one of the prettiest Georgian townscapes in England. Truro's skyline is dominated by the three spires of its magnificent cathedral, built of Bath stone and granite and completed in 1910. It was the first Anglican cathedral to be built since St Paul's in London.

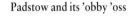

Padstow and its 'obby 'oss

Before the motor car, the only way to get from one side of Padstow to the other was by boat across the bay, or the long way round, by pony and trap! Before the advent of the railway, Padstow was the premier port on the north Cornwall coast, but the gradual silting up of the River Camel led to its decline. Today it is a popular holiday resort. Highlight of the calendar comes on May Day with the 'obby 'oss festivities: in a ritual that began in pagan times, the heathen god, represented by an 'oss, is led through the streets by the teaser and followed by dancers in white.

Lanhydrock

Built for Baron Robartes in the seventeenth century, this fine house was largely rebuilt after a fire in 1881. The gatehouse, however, survived (*right*). The interior of the house provides a fascinating insight into the way a late nineteenth-century house was run. It passed to the National Trust in 1953. In the garden are several urns by Louis Ballin, goldsmith to Louis XIV.

TINTAGEL – LAND OF THE WINTER KING

Every mile of the Cornish coastal path is steeped in history, none more so than the one which skirts round Tintagel Head, seat of the Celtic kings and legendary birthplace of King Arthur. There is no conclusive proof that Arthur ever existed, but if he did, there can be no finer site for his court of the Round Table. In 1136, Geoffrey of Monmouth was the first to write of Arthur in his *History of the Kings of Britain*. As he tells the tale, Arthur was conceived at Tintagel by Igraine during a night of passion with King Uther Pendragon. Monmouth's story continues with the creation of the knights of the Round Table and the tragic love affair of Guinevere and Sir Lancelot, and concludes with the rebellion of Mordred and the return of the sword Excalibur to the lake at Dozmary Pool. In the nineteenth century, Alfred Tennyson added greatly to the myth with his *Morte d'Arthur*. Cynics may shrug at the myth, but no one who has taken the perilous path down the steep flight of steps that leads to a bridge and finally to the stormy headland can doubt the legend: at Tintagel, seeing is believing.

King Arthur (Hall of Chivalry)

The last outpost of a Cornish king?

The ruin that remains today, a fragment of a curtain wall, is a Norman structure, but pottery finds – tiny pieces from over 250 vessels made for wine and olive oil, including bowls from Turkey, dishes from Carthage, oil jars from Tunisia and amphoras from Cilicia – indicate fifth- or sixth-century occupation. There is evidence of a Cornish warrior king who defended British Cornwall against the Saxons in the fifth century.

Tintagel's Norman church

The cliff-top Norman church is guardian of one of Cornwall's rare Roman relics, a fourth-century milestone.

Tintagel Post Office

To all appearances this looks just like another quaint, slate cottage, but in fact it is a rare early-fifteenth-century manor house whose central hall is open to the roof timbers. It was used from 1844 to 1892 as the letter-receiving office for the district. Mail was brought by foot from the coaching stage at Camelford, six miles away.

Weathering the storm

In spring wild primroses cover the banks on the steep descent from Tintagel village to the headland.

Hall of Chivalry

The custard magnate, Arthurian devotee Frederick Thomas Glasscock, set out to build the ultimate tribute to his hero. The result is two halls decorated with over fifty kinds of Cornish stone, specially commissioned oil paintings and seventy-three stained glass windows telling the story of the knights of the Round Table.

The Newlyn School

Newlyn is Cornwall's major fishing port, supplying the EC markets with the finest-quality fish. Its visitor appeal, however, lies in its artistic connections. The Newlyn School of Painting, founded by Laura Knight at the beginning of the century, was famous for its portrayal of the traditional way of life.

The wooden roundhouse, Sennen Cove

This building, which once contained rope and chain windlass for hauling boats ashore, is now a craft centre. It is a stone's throw from Whitesand Bay, one of England's finest surfing beaches.

St Michael's Mount

One of the south-west's most famous sights, St Michael's Mount was once joined to the mainland and the remains of a petrified forest have been found beneath the surrounding sea. Now at high tide the Mount becomes an island. It takes its name from a day in AD 495 when the archangel St Michael is said to have appeared to a group of fishermen. Another legend claims that this was once the home of Cormoran, the giant slain by Jack the Giant Killer. The discovery of a skeleton over two metres long in the castle chapel suggests that the story may be more than legend.

Relic of prehistory

The significance of Men-an-tol, a curious stone standing between two uprights, near Lanyon, is lost in the mists of time. Legend has it that to cure aches and pains you must climb through the ring nine times against the sun.

*Land's End:
the westernmost
point in England*

The Cornish language commemorated

Cornwall's ancient Celtic language survived until Tudor times when English, the language of commerce, took over; but in the late eighteenth century Cornish speakers could still be found in remote districts. A slate plaque in the fishing village of Mousehole commemorates one of the last, Dolly Pentreath, a fishwife, who died in 1777.

Davy lamp

For over a century Penzance was the mining centre of the Penwith peninsula. In Market Square there is a statue to the town's most famous son, Sir Humphry Davy, inventor of the miners' safety lamp. The lamp replaced the tallow candle miners carried in their hats and thus lessened the risk of an explosion from gas combustion.

THE PENWITH PENINSULA
A 'TOE' IN THE ATLANTIC

The ancient hundred of Penwith revels in its existence as the farthest-flung corner of England, with little but ocean between it and the Americas. The Cornish hundreds, or territorial divisions, are likely to pre-date Norman times, when they were first recorded. At the most westerly point in mainland England, which the Romans aptly named Belerion (meaning 'seat of storms'), the 'Land's End Experience' tourist attraction has been sited. Here, the Cornish coastal path leaves the Atlantic and turns east along magnificent cliff scenery.

Period parlour

The countryside around Zennor was heavily populated from 3000 BC and is rich in archaeological sites and remains. Zennor's Wayside Museum, founded in 1935 by Colonel Freddie Hirst, contains implements and relics covering every aspect of local life from early 4000 BC to the 1930s.

Contemporary art in St Ives

The Barbara Hepworth Museum in St Ives houses a permanent exhibition of the sculptor's work. Hepworth lived in this building from 1949 until her death in 1975, and the sculptures, which spill out into the garden, are arranged in positions personally chosen by the artist.

Theatre by the sea

The Minack Open Air Theatre at Porthcurno, with its unrivalled setting, was the inspired creation of Rowena Cade, who began her work on the site in 1923. Of the first performance, *The Tempest* in 1932, the *Times* reported: 'Short of securing an island and wrecking a ship on its coast, there could be no more ideal setting'. Professional companies perform here throughout the summer.

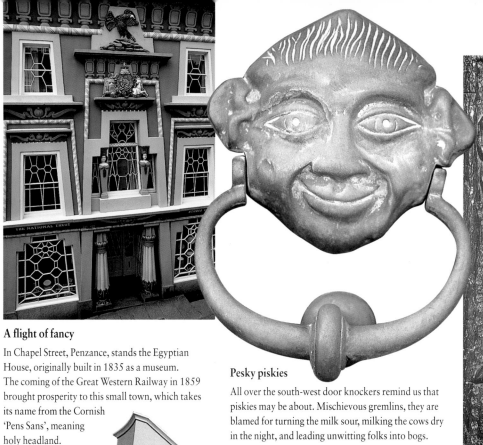

A flight of fancy

In Chapel Street, Penzance, stands the Egyptian House, originally built in 1835 as a museum. The coming of the Great Western Railway in 1859 brought prosperity to this small town, which takes its name from the Cornish 'Pens Sans', meaning holy headland.

Pesky piskies

All over the south-west door knockers remind us that piskies may be about. Mischievous gremlins, they are blamed for turning the milk sour, milking the cows dry in the night, and leading unwitting folks into bogs.

Mermaid myth

Carved into a bench end in Zennor's church is the figure of a mermaid. In the Middle Ages, when Cornish mystery plays were performed, the mermaid was used to explain the two natures of Christ: she was both human and fish, He was both man and God. Legend has it that in Zennor a beautiful mermaid was drawn to the church by the singing of one Matthew Trewhella. He returned to the sea with her and his despairing father had the bench end carved in the vain hope that she would return his son.

THE TATE IN CORNWALL

The new Tate Gallery in St Ives, sister to the London Tate, houses changing displays of twentieth-century art related to Cornwall on a splendid sea-front site above Porthmeor beach. St Ives is well known as a centre for artists: it all began in the nineteenth century when Turner, Sickert and Whistler were among the many to be captivated by the Mediterranean climate and the translucent Cornish light. More recently, Laura Knight, Dod Procter, Ben Nicholson and Barbara Hepworth have been prominent in continuing the tradition. Barbara Hepworth donated much of her work to the museum, and her own garden, which is also in St Ives, has been transformed into a sculpture garden.

Dead men tell no tales

Kynance, now a favourite of holidaymakers, was once the haunt of wreckers; 400 shipwreck victims are buried in its churchyard. The great peaks, upon which so many vessels foundered, are made of serpentine.

Cornish courage

In the fishing village of Cadgwith, thatch is secured against gales by heavy chain. In 1907, its lifeboat braved raging seas to rescue 227 men from the ship *Suevic*. When the weather is less turbulent, visitors can enjoy boat trips from here.

Come-to-Good

This name is a corruption of the Cornish 'Cwn-t-coit' meaning 'combe by the dwelling in the wood'. The charming cottage pictured here, near Feock, was built as a Quaker meeting house in 1710.

SOUTH CORNWALL
TALES OF TREACHERY, CUNNING AND BRAVERY

Turn the clock back 200 years and picture this: a storm-tossed, moonless night, waves crashing against the harbour wall; at sea a flashing lantern and on shore a Customs official on the rampage, determined to catch the smugglers red-handed. Drenched to the skin, he is unaware that the smugglers have access to a secret tunnel as he beats on the door of their cliff-top home. By the time the door is opened, the smugglers have already returned to their beds.

Tap a Cornish wall, they say, and you'll find a secret passage. In days past, the survival of entire communities depended on the harvest from the sea. When the catch failed, they faced starvation. Not surprisingly, smuggling became a way of life. The whole village would often be involved, for it took two teams, one at sea and one ashore, to haul the booty up the cliff to the waiting wagons.

There are tales of darker deeds too, of cattle with lanterns tied to their horns and driven on to the beach. Ships at sea would mistake the lights for vessels safely anchored and, misguided, be driven on to the rocks and sure destruction. The Cornish had a prayer in those days: 'We pray Lord, not that wrecks should occur, but if they do, that Thou drive them here for the benefit of the poor inhabitants.'

Exotica in an English garden

At Trebah, four miles from Falmouth, the steeply wooded ravine garden falls sixty metres from the eighteenth-century house to a private beach on the Helford River. Here, sub-tropical tree ferns mingle with giant gunnera against a backdrop of rhododendrons. Streams cascade over waterfalls to ponds where giant Koi carp and exotic water plants flourish.

A light on the Lizard

The most southerly point on the British mainland, the Lizard did not have a regular lighthouse until 1752. It was from here that the Spanish Armada was first sighted in 1588. The present lighthouse is the most powerful in the British Isles and with clear visibility, can be seen for over forty miles.

A notorious past

In the eighteenth century, the fishing village of Polperro was renowned for smuggling, with the entire population in league against Customs and Excise. During the Napoleonic Wars shipowners were encouraged to carry arms and in peacetime these were used by smuggling vessels to great effect against the forces of law and order.

Mevagissey ducks

In the heyday of the pilchard (known as Mevagissey ducks), August was the month when the entire village would stand by, ready for the cry of 'Hevva! Hevva!' at the first sight of the long-awaited shoals. Apart from being the staple diet, pilchards provided oil for light and fuel. With little demand for them elsewhere in England, the community was dependent on trade with Italy and Spain, where they were in great demand during Lent. Mevagissey enjoyed great rivalry with the nearby Gorran Haven which boasted seven quays. But the Mevagissey shipbuilders were superior, famed for their fine, fast sailing luggers.

A poignant memorial

Sunset at Mawgan Porth, where there is evidence of an early medieval settlement. The churchyard of St Mawgan has a poignant memorial to nine men and a boy who died of exposure on a life raft when their ship sank in heavy seas in 1846.

No hiding place

Aesthetically pleasing, these delightful roundhouses dotted across Veryan Bay from Dodman Point were constructed out of 'practical' considerations: it was believed that the devil liked to hide in corners.

Devil's Frying Pan, near Cadgwith

Centuries of pounding seas have carved out this arch where the sea is like a seething cauldron.

Troy Town

Immortalised in the novels of Sir Arthur Quiller-Couch, who wrote under the *nom de plume* of 'Q', Fowey has been a busy port since the days when its fearless seafarers were known as 'Fowey Gallants'.

Shipwreck saviour

At Helston there is a memorial to Henry Trengrouse, inventor of the rocket apparatus, for communication between stranded ships and the shore.

Mullion Cove

The entire Lizard Peninsula is a defined area of outstanding natural beauty. Mullion Cove was a busy port in 1337, and was let for £1 a year. The present solid granite pier was rebuilt by the National Trust in 1962. It looks out to Mullion Island, a breeding ground for sea birds.

LOCATION MAP

CORNWALL

1 Bedruthan Steps
2 Bolventor
3 Boscastle
4 Botallack
5 Cadgwith
6 Chysauster
7 Feock
8 Fowey
9 Gwennap
10 Helston
11 Kynance
12 Land's End
13 Lanhydrock
14 Madron
15 Mevagissey
16 Mawgan Porth

17 Mount Edgcumbe
18 Mousehole
19 Mullion
20 Newlyn
21 Polperro
22 Port Isaac
23 Porthcurno
24 Rough Tor
25 St Michael's Mount
26 Saltash
27 Sennen
28 Tintagel
29 Trebah
30 Trerice
31 Veryan
32 Zennor

Lundy

Exmoor

50 56
49
48
59
33

57
Barnstaple

41

Devon

River Exe

53
51
Okehampton
39
Exeter
45 40
Dartmoor 54
35 47
3 58 44
28 38
Launceston
Bodmin Moor
55
22
24 *River Dart*
2
1 Padstow 37
Torquay
Bodmin 42
Newquay 26 Paignton
30 *Cornwall* 13
Totnes 36
8 21 Plymouth 46
17 43
Truro
15 34
31
32 *Helford River* *Burgh Island* 52
St Ives 9
6
4 14 Penzance Falmouth
20 29
12 10
23 25
18 16
27 19
11 5

The Lizard

Isles of Scilly

DEVON

33 Arlington
34 Bigbury-on-Sea
35 Bowerman's Nose
36 Brixham
37 Buckland-in-the-Moor
38 Budleigh Salterton
39 Castle Drogo
40 Chagford
41 Clovelly
42 Cockington
43 Dartmouth
44 Exmouth
45 Gidleigh
46 Harberton

47 Haytor Rock
48 Ilfracombe
49 Lynmouth
50 Lynton
51 Ottery St Mary
52 Salcombe
53 Shute
54 Sidmouth
55 Vixen Tor
56 Watersmeet
57 Westward Ho!
58 Widecombe-
in-the-Moor
59 Woolacombe